Cataraqui United Church Cemetery

The Grave Whisperer, Volume 7

Angeline Gallant

Published by Angeline Gallant, 2023.

While every precaution has been taken in the preparation of this book, the publisher assumes no responsibility for errors or omissions, or for damages resulting from the use of the information contained herein.

CATARAQUI UNITED CHURCH CEMETERY

First edition. April 5, 2023.

Copyright © 2023 Angeline Gallant.

ISBN: 979-8215679791

Written by Angeline Gallant.

Also by Angeline Gallant

A Dragon's Diary
Dreaming of Dragons

Calling Her Heart
Whisper of the Heart
No Turning Back
Forsake Me Not
Hear My Cry
Calling Her Heart Boxed Set Volumes 1-4

FORGET ME NOT
Victoria, Ontario's Babies 1894 - 1895

Keeper Of Secrets
A Lady's Secret

Midnight's Awakening

Heart of the Storm
Walking Through The Storm
Walking Through The Storm
Heart of the Storm

Secrets of the Underworld
Deklan's Dragons

Tell My Story Collection
Tell My Story: England 1852

The Grave Whisperer
Cataraqui United Church Cemetery
Wedding Bells in Kingston, Ontario, Canada 1923
St. Paul's Anglican Churchyard Kingston, Ontario, Canada A-B
St. Paul's Anglican Churchyard, Kingston, Ontario, Canada C - D
St. Paul's Anglican Churchyard, Kingston, Ontario, Canada G - H
St. Paul's Anglican Churchyard, Kingston, Ontario, Canada J - N
St. Paul's Anglican Churchyard, Kingston, Ontario, Canada O - R
St. Paul's Anglican Churchyard, Kingston, Ontario, Canada S - T
St. Paul's Anglican Churchyard, Kingston, Ontario T - Z
Small Graveyards & Burial Grounds: Kingston, Ontario, Canada
Cataraqui United Church Cemetery 1
Cataraqui United Church Cemetery 2
Cataraqui United Church Cemetery 3
Cataraqui United Church Cemetery 4
Cataraqui United Church Cemetery 5
Beth Israel Cemetery

The Wolf Whisperer Series
The Cry of the Wolf
Captured Heart
Journey of the Heart
Wolf Whisperer volumes 1 & 2
Endless White
The Wolf Whisperer Volumes 1-4
The Wolf Whisperer volumes 1 & 2

Standalone
Winds of Change vol 1-3

Watch for more at https://www.goodreads.com/author/show/ 19703964.Angeline_Gallant.

ALEXANDER IRWIN[1]

Alexander was born in Ontario in January 1866.

He was 5 years old when British Columbia joined the confederation in 1871.

Alexander was 17 years old when the mining boom in Northern Ontario took place in 1883.

He was 32 years old when he married Bertha in Kingston, Ontario on April 7, 1898.

Alexander was 40 years old when Ontario Hydro was established in 1906.

He was 68 years old when the Dionne Quintuplets were born in 1934.

Alexander was 76 years old when he passed away in 1942. He was Irish and Methodist.

ANNIE E. (PURDY) IRWIN[2]

Annie was born in Ontario in September 1867. She was German. She was three years old when British Columbia joined the confederation in 1871.

In 1881 she was 13 years old and living in Portland, Ontario.

She was 17 years old when her father passed away in 1885.

Annie was 42 years old when she married George on April 10, 1920 in Frontenac, Ontario.

She was 91 years old when she passed away in 1959. Annie was Methodist.

BERTHA (GORDON) IRWIN[3]

Bertha was born in Ontario in 1867.

She was 16 years old when the mining boom in Northern Ontario took place in 1883.

Bertha was 24 years old when her father passed away in 1891.

She was 31 years old when she married Alexander in Kingston, Ontario on March 7, 1898.

Bertha was 39 years old when Ontario Hydro was established in 1906.

She was 61 years old when her mother passed away in 1928.

Bertha was 73 years old when she passed away in 1940. She was Scott/Irish and Methodist.

GEORGE IRWIN[4]

George was born in Ontario in 1868. He was Irish.

He was three years old when British Columbia joined the confederation in 1871.

George was 15 years old when the mining boom in Northern Ontario began in 1883.

He was 38 years old when Ontario Hydro was established in 1906.

George was 41 years old when his father passed away in 1909.

He was 42 years old when he married Annie on April 10, 1910.

George was 62 years old when his mother passed away in 1930.

He was 66 years old when the Dionne Quintuplets were born in 1934.

George was 85 years old when he passed away in 1953. He was Methodist.

KATHLEEN THERESA (ORSER) IRWIN[5]

Kathleen was born in the United States in 1893.

She was three years old when Pleggy vs. Ferguson took place in 1896.

By the time she was eight years old, she was living in Frontenac, Ontario.

Kathleen was 13 years old when Ontario Hydro was established in 1906.

William and Kathleen were married in 1915 when she was 22 years old.

Kathleen was 24 years old when she gave birth to a stillborn daughter on November 24, 1917. She passed away three days later on November 27th. Kathleen was Dutch and Methodist.

WILLIAM FRANKLIN IRWIN[6]

William was born in April 1888. He was Irish.

He was 17 years old when Ontario Hydro was founded in 1906.

William was 27 years old when he married Kathleen on September 4, 1915 in Kingston, Ontario.

He was 29 years old when his wife passed away in 1917.

William was 31 years old when he married Mildred Florence Graham on November 22, 1919 in Kingston, Ontario.

He was 45 years old when his father passed away in 1933.

William was 48 years old when his mother passed away in 1937.

He was 53 years old when he passed away in 1942. William was Methodist.

CALEB JACKSON[7]

Caleb was born on September 4, 1848.

He was five years old when he passed away on November 8, 1853.

JANE ELEANOR (SPOONER) JACKSON[8]

Jane was born on March 19, 1839 in Canada. She was German.

In 1851, Jane was 11 years old and living in Storrington, Ontario.

Jane was 29 years old when she married William on July 23, 1867 in Frontenac, Ontario. He was 50 years old and a widower.

She was 31 years old when British Columbia joined the confederation in 1871.

Jane was 43 years old when the mining boom in northern Ontario took place in 1883.

She was 52 years old when her husband passed away in 1891.

Jane was 60 years old when she passed away on May 3, 1899. She was Methodist.

JOSHUA V. H. JACKSON[9]

Joshua was born on April 24, 1846 in Kingston, Ontario.
He was 19 years old when he passed away on April 17, 1866.

MARY (POWLEY) JACKSON[10]

Mary was born on January 28, 1823.

She was nine years old when The Factory Act was passed in 1833.

Mary was 19 years old when Dickens' "A Christmas Carol" was first published in 1843.

In 1851, she was 28 years old and living in Kingston, Ontario.

Mary was 31 years old when the Crimean War took place in 1853.

She was 43 years old when she passed away on April 21, 1866. Mary was Methodist.

WILLIAM JACKSON JR.[11]

William was born on July 15, 1817 in Kingston, Ontario. He was German.

In 1851 he was 33 years old and working as a blacksmith. Previously he had been a carriage maker.

William was 36 years old when his son, Caleb, passed away in 1853.

He was 48 years old when his wife, Mary, passed away in 1866.

William was 49 years old when Ontario was founded on July 1, 1867.

He was 50 years old when he married Jane Eleanor Spooner on July 23, 1867 in Frontenac, Ontario. She was 29 years old.

William was 53 years old when British Columbia joined the confederation in 1871.

He was 65 years old when the mining boom in northern Ontario began in 1883.

William was 73 years old when he passed away on April 15, 1891. He was Methodist.

ALBERT HAROLD JOHNSON[12]

Albert was born on December 31, 1896 in Loughborough, Ontario. He was German.

He was nine years old when Ontario Hydro was established in 1906.

Albert was 20 years old when he was drafted into WWI in 1917.

Verna Agnes and Albert were married on November 11, 1920 in Jefferson, New York.

He was 25 years old when his wife passed away on October 6, 1922.

Arthur was 26 years old when he married Eva Bell on September 1, 1923.

He was 37 years old when the Dionne Quintuplets were born in 1934.

Arthur was 40 years old when the Neutrality Act was passed in 1937.

He was 42 years old when he passed away in 1939.

EMMA JANE (RUTTAN) JOHNSON[13]

Emma was born on June 30, 1862 in Pittsburgh, Ontario.
She was four years old when Ontario was founded on July 1, 1867.

Emma was 17 years old when she married James Henry Berry in Kingston, Ontario on April 28, 1880.

She was 24 years old when her husband passed away in 1887.

Emma was 43 years old when Ontario Hydro was established in 1906.

She was 49 years old when the Girl Scouts was founded in 1912.

Emma was 71 years old when the Dionne Quintuplets were born in 1934.

She was 76 years old when her son, Albert Harold, passed away in 1939.

Emma was 79 years old when her husband, John, passed away in 1941.

She was 93 years old when she passed away in 1956.

JOHN B. JOHNSON/JOHNSTON[14]

John was born in Kingston, Ontario in 1859.

He was seven years old when Ontario was founded on July 1, 1867.

John was 11 years old when British Columbia joined the confederation in 1871.

He was 31 years old when he married Emma Jane in Inverary, Ontario on December 9, 1890.

John was 37 years old when his son, Albert Harold, was born in 1896.

He was 46 years old when Ontario Hydro was established in 1906.

John was 74 years old when the Dionne Quintuplets were born in 1934.

He was 79 years old when his son, Albert Harold, passed away in 1939.

John was 82 years old when he passed away on December 19, 1941. He was German and Methodist.

JOHN WESLEY JOHNSON[15]

John was born in 1926.

He was eight years old when the Dionne Quintuplets were born in 1934.

John was 56 years old when the Canada Act was passed in 1982.

He was 62 years old when he passed away in 1988.

THOMAS JOHNSON[16]

T homas was 52 years old when he passed away in 1953.

ELIZABETH JOY[17]

E lizabeth was 46 years old when she passed away on August 1, 1834.

JOHN JOY[18]

John was 96 years old when he passed away on September 24, 1867.

EMMA ADELAIDE (SINGLETON) KEMP[19]

Elma was born in Kingston, Ontario on April 26, 1876. She was Irish. She was six years old when the mining boom began in northern Ontario in 1883.

Elma was 23 years old when she married William John Kemp in Kingston, Ontario on August 22, 1899.

She was 29 years old when Ontario Hydro was established in 1906.

Elma was 65 years old when her husband passed away in 1941.

She was 74 years old when she passed away in Toronto, Ontario on January 11, 1951.

WILLIAM KEMP[20]

William was born in Kingston, Ontario on October 27, 1875.
He was seven years old when the mining boom in northern Ontario began in 1883.

William was 23 years old when he married Elma in Kingston, Ontario on August 22, 1899.

He was 30 years old when Ontario Hydro was established in 1906.

William was 53 years old when his mother passed away in 1929.

He was 55 years old when his father passed away in 1930.

William was 58 years old when the Dionne Quintuplets were born in 1934.

He was 65 years old when he passed away on May 4, 1941 in Toronto, Ontario.

PETER KNAPP[21]

Peter was born in Kingston, Frontenac, Upper Canada, British Colonial America in 1812.

He was 55 years old when Ontario was founded on July 1, 1867.

Peter was 59 years old when British Columbia joined the confederation in 1871.

He was 71 years old when the mining boom in northern Ontario began in 1883.

Peter was 77 years old when he passed away on January 19, 1889. He was Irish, Methodist, and a farmer.

SARAH (GUESS) KNAPP[22]

Sarah was born in 1818. She was Irish.

She was 49 years old when Ontario was founded on July 1, 1867.

Sarah was 53 years old when British Columbia joined the confederation in 1871.

She was 65 years old when she passed away on July 24, 1883. Sarah was Methodist.

SOPHIA ROSSIMAN (BOOTH) LAKE[23]

Sophia was born in 1848 in Lennox and Addington, Ontario. She was 16 years old when her father passed away in 1864.

Sophia was 21 years old when she married Edwin on November 26, 1869 in Odessa, Ontario.

She was 79 years old when she passed away in York, Ontario on November 26, 1927.

SAMUEL LATTEMORE[24]

Samuel was 52 years old when he passed away on December 26, 1847.

ANNIE (MAVETY) LAWRENCE[25]

Annie was born on February 20, 1857 in Kingston, Ontario. She was nine years old when Ontario was founded on July 1, 1867.

Annie was 13 years old when British Columbia joined the confederation in 1871.

She was 34 years old when she married William Asa Clothier on April 22, 1891 in Kingston, Ontario.

Annie was 40 years old when her husband passed away in 1897.

She was 46 years old when she married Elias Lawrence Sr., a 74-year-old widower on October 7, 1903 in Leeds and Grenville, Ontario.

Annie was 48 years old when Ontario Hydro was established in 1908.

She was 54 years old when her husband passed away in 1911.

Annie was 76 years old when the Dionne Quintuplets were born in 1934.

She was 81 years old when she passed away on April 17, 1938 in Kemptville, Ontario. Annie is buried in Kingston, Ontario.

CATHERINE JANE (POWLEY) LAWSON[26]

Catherine was born on September 8, 1843 in Kepler, Ontario. She was Irish and German.

She was 23 years old when Ontario was founded on July 1, 1867. Catherine married Joseph Lawson that same year.

Catherine was 27 years old when British Columbia joined the confederation in 1871.

She was 39 years old when the mining boom in northern Ontario began in 1883.

Catherine was 55 years old when her mother passed away in 1899.

She was 57 years old when her father passed away in 1901.

Catherine was 62 years old when Ontario Hydro was established in 1906.

She was 73 years old when her husband passed away in 1917.

Catherine was 82 years old when she passed away on June 18, 1926.

ELEANOR "ELLEN" (McNAMARA) LAWSON[27]

Ellen was born in Kingston, Ontario on March 27, 1844. She was Irish.

She was 40 years old when the Canadian Pacific Railroad was completed in 1885.

Ellen was 67 years old when she passed away on August 17, 1911 in Kingston, Ontario. She was Methodist.

JOSEPH LAWSON[28]

Joseph was born in Elton, England on October 16, 1844.

He was 22 years old when he married Catherine Jane in Ontario in 1867.

Joseph was 26 years old and living in Loughborough in 1871.

By 1881 he was living in Kingston, Ontario.

Joseph was 40 years old when the Canadian Pacific Railway was completed in 1885.

He was 57 years old when his father passed away in 1902.

Joseph was 69 years old when Canada entered into WWI in 1914.

He was 72 years old when he passed away on March 21, 1917. Joseph was Methodist and a farmer.

PVT. MILFORD PARKINSON LAWSON[29]

Milford was born in Canada in 1879.

He was two years old and living in Kingston, Ontario in 1881.

Milford was six years old when the Canadian Pacific Railroad was completed in 1885.

He was 38 years old when his father passed away in 1917.

Milford was 42 years old when he married Florence in Kingston, Ontario on August 20, 1921. Florence was 45 years old.

He was 47 years old when his mother passed away in 1926.

Milford served as a private in the 103rd Battalion.

He was 59 years old when he passed away on March 23, 1938.

WILLIAM LAWSON[30]

William was born in Cropwell Butler, England on June 20, 1842. He was two years old when his brother, Joseph, was born in 1844.

William was 39 years old when his mother passed away in 1881.

He was 42 years old when the Canadian Pacific Railway was completed in 1885.

By this time, William was living in Kingston, Ontario where he worked as a carriage maker.

William was 59 years old when his father passed away in 1902.

He was 60 years old when the Wright brothers made their first flight in 1903.

William was 69 years old when his wife passed away in 1911.

He was 70 years old when he passed away in Loughborough, Ontario on October 13, 1912. William was Methodist and a carriage maker at the time of his death.

SARAH M. (LEARD) PURDY[31]

Sarah was 77 years old when she passed away on February 28, 1889.

MARY (MOOERS) LEATHERLAND[32]

Mary was 72 years old when she passed away on August 20, 1893.

ANNA LEONARD[33]

Anna was 19 years old when she passed away on March 13, 1865.

NATHANIEL LEONARD[34]

Nathaniel was born in Middleborough, Massachusetts in 1766.
He was 17 years old when his father passed away in 1783.

Nathaniel was 22 years old when he married Elisabeth in Middleborough, Massachusetts on March 20, 1788.

He was 44 years old when his mother passed away in 1810.

Nathaniel was 62 years old when he passed away in 1828.

RUSSELL SEYMORE LOVELACE[35]

Russell was born in Ontario in March 1900.
He was 14 years old when Canada entered into WWI in 1914.
Russell was 52 years old when his father passed away in 1953.
He was 64 years old when he passed away in 1964.

SHERWIN EDWARD LUNN[36]

Sherwin was born in 1913.

He was 56 years old when Neil Armstrong became the first man to step onto the moon in 1969.

Sherwin was 86 years old when he passed away in 1999.

BENJAMIN MABEE[37]

Benjamin was born in Ernestown, Ontario on August 8, 1824.
He was 24 years old when he married Sarah Jane in Kingston on August 8, 1848.

Benjamin was 48 years old when he married Amanda Martha in Murray, Ontario on October 8, 1872.

He was 60 years old when the Canadian Pacific Railway was completed in 1885.

Benjamin was 61 years old when his father passed away in 1886.

He was 63 years old when his mother passed away in 1888.

Benjamin was 78 years old when he passed away on October 29, 1902 in Odessa, Ontario.

DANIEL MABEE[38]

D aniel was born on August 23, 1853.
He was a year old when he passed away on May 24, 1855.

MILLARD WILLIAM MABEE M.D.

Millard was born in Kingston in 1856.
He worked as a P. S. teacher.

Millard was 28 years old when the Canadian Pacific Railroad was completed in 1885.

Addie and Millard were married in Athol, Ontario on March 18, 1891 when he was 35 years old and Addie was 25.

Millard was 43 years old and living in Riverside, California in 1900.

He was 46 years old when his father passed away in 1902.

Millard was a physician when he passed away in Riverside, California on June 10, 1903. He is buried in Kingston.

REBECCA E. MABEE[39]

Rebecca was born on May 15, 1858.
She was two years old when she passed away on June 5, 1860.

SARAH JANE (DAVID) MABEE[40]

Sarah was born on March 11, 1832.

She was 16 years old when she married Benjamin in Kingston, Ontario on August 8, 1848.

Sarah was 23 years old when her one-year-old son, Daniel, passed away in 1855.

She was 28 years old when her two-year-old daughter, Rebecca, passed away in 1860.

Sarah was 52 years old when the Canadian Pacific Railway was completed in 1885.

She was 70 years old when her husband passed away in 1902.

Sarah was 71 years old when her son, Millard William, passed away in 1903.

She was 93 years old when she passed away in Ottawa, Ontario on January 29, 1924. Sarah is buried in Kingston, Ontario. She was Welsh.

WILLIAM CLARK MacARTHUR[41]

William was born on April 6, 1881 in London, Ontario. He passed away on July 25, 1881 and is buried in Kingston, Ontario.

ANNIE MAUD (BARNUM) MacDONALD[42]

Annie was born on May 2, 1907.
She was 37 years old when WWII ended in 1945.
Annie was 91 years old when she passed away in 1999.

GEORGE ALBERT MacDONALD[43]

George was born in Kingston, Ontario in 1910.

He was four years old when Canada entered into WWI in 1914.

George was 46 years old when his father passed away in 1956.

He was 61 years old when the Canadian government officially adopted a policy on multiculturalism in 1971.

George was 67 years old when he passed away in Kingston in 1977.

THELMA MAY (WRIGHT) MADDEN[44]

Thelma was born in Collins Bay, Ontario on May 4, 1899.

She was 35 years old when her father passed away in 1934. Thelma was 37 years old when her mother passed away in 1937.

She was 94 years old when she passed away in 1994. Thelma was Methodist.

ELSIE E. (CUDDY) MAHONEY[45]

E lsie was born in 1919.

She was 47 years old when her father passed away in 1966.

Elsie was 50 years old when Neil Armstrong became the first person to walk on the moon in 1969.

She was 55 years old when her mother passed away in 1977.

Elsie was 63 years old when she and her husband both passed away in 1982.

GORDON WILLIAM MAHONEY[46]

Gordon was born in Toronto, Ontario in 1916. He was 66 years old when he passed away in 1982.

EMILY MARTIN[47]

Emily was born in 1885. She passed away the same year and is buried in Kingston, Ontario.

ISABELLA MARTIN[48]

Isabella was 60 years old when she passed away on March 28, 1879.

JOHN MARTIN[49]

John was born in 1828.

He was 51 years old when his wife, Isabella, passed away in 1879.

John was 56 years old when he passed away in 1884.

JOHN WESLEY MARTIN[50]

John was born in 1855.

He was 24 years old when his mother passed away in 1879.

John was 29 years old when his father passed away in 1884.

He was 72 years old when he passed away in 1927. John Wesley was Methodist.

MARY ELLEN MARTIN[51]

Mary was born in 1866.

She was four years old when she passed away on January 13, 1871.

MARY HIMES (JACKSON) MARTIN[52]

Mary was born in 1866, the same year her mother passed away. She was German.

She was 18 years old when she married John Wesley in Kingston, Ontario on May 21, 1884. He was 25 years old.

Mary was 19 years old when her baby daughter, Emily, passed away in 1885.

She was 25 years old when her father passed away in 1891.

Mary was 60 years old when her husband passed away in 1927. She passed away the following year. Mary was Methodist.

[1] https://www.wikitree.com/genealogy/Irwin-Family-Tree-6637[1]

[2] https://www.wikitree.com/wiki/Purdy-3747[2]

[3] https://www.wikitree.com/genealogy/Gordon-Family-Tree-19143

[4] https://www.wikitree.com/wiki/Irwin-6638[3]

[5] https://www.wikitree.com/wiki/Orser-534

[6] https://www.wikitree.com/wiki/Irwin-6680[4]

[7] https://www.wikitree.com/wiki/Jackson-55199

[8] https://www.wikitree.com/wiki/Spooner-1760

[9] https://www.wikitree.com/wiki/Jackson-37168

[10] https://www.wikitree.com/wiki/Powley-347

[11] https://www.wikitree.com/wiki/Jackson-37170

[12] https://www.wikitree.com/wiki/Johnson-93157

[13] https://www.wikitree.com/wiki/Ruttan-384

[14] https://www.wikitree.com/wiki/Johnson-125363

[15] https://www.wikitree.com/wiki/Johnson-134845

[16] https://www.wikitree.com/wiki/Johnson-134846

[17] https://www.wikitree.com/wiki/Joy-2701

[18] https://www.wikitree.com/wiki/Joy-2871

[19] https://www.wikitree.com/wiki/Singleton-4973

[20] https://www.wikitree.com/wiki/Kemp-4251

[21] https://www.wikitree.com/wiki/Knapp-7182

[22] https://www.wikitree.com/wiki/Guess-899

[23] https://www.wikitree.com/wiki/Booth-11903

[24] https://www.wikitree.com/wiki/Lattemore-10

[25] https://www.wikitree.com/wiki/Mavety-4

[26] https://www.wikitree.com/wiki/Powley-304

[27] https://www.wikitree.com/wiki/McNamara-4383

1. https://www.wikitree.com/genealogy/Wright-Family-Tree-60404

2. https://www.wikitree.com/genealogy/Purdy-Family-Tree-3747

3. https://www.wikitree.com/genealogy/Irwin-Family-Tree-6638

4. https://www.findagrave.com/memorial/18346824/caleb-jackson

[28] https://www.wikitree.com/wiki/Lawson-13495

[29] https://www.wikitree.com/wiki/Lawson-13497

[30] https://www.wikitree.com/wiki/Lawson-13501

[31] https://www.wikitree.com/wiki/Leard-242

[32] https://www.wikitree.com/wiki/Mooers-365

[33] https://www.wikitree.com/wiki/Leonard-14606

[34] https://www.wikitree.com/wiki/Leonard-7878

[35] https://www.wikitree.com/wiki/Lovelace-1072

[36] https://www.wikitree.com/wiki/Lunn-1405

[37] https://www.wikitree.com/wiki/Mabee-414

[38] https://www.wikitree.com/wiki/Mabee-415

[39] https://www.wikitree.com/wiki/Mabee-417

[40] https://www.wikitree.com/wiki/David-4242

[41] https://www.wikitree.com/wiki/MacArthur-838

[42] https://www.wikitree.com/wiki/Barnum-6835

[43] https://www.wikitree.com/wiki/MacDonald-10457

[44] https://www.wikitree.com/wiki/Wright-61785

[45] https://www.wikitree.com/wiki/Cuddy-264

[46] https://www.wikitree.com/wiki/Mahoney-3820

[47] https://www.wikitree.com/wiki/Martin-84692

[48] https://www.wikitree.com/wiki/Unknown-640311

[49] https://www.wikitree.com/wiki/Martin-84693

[50] https://www.wikitree.com/wiki/Martin-84694

[51] https://www.wikitree.com/wiki/Martin-84695

[52] https://www.wikitree.com/wiki/Jackson-55322

Don't miss out!

Visit the website below and you can sign up to receive emails whenever Angeline Gallant publishes a new book. There's no charge and no obligation.

https://books2read.com/r/B-A-QGSI-UCPHC

BOOKS2READ

Connecting independent readers to independent writers.

Also by Angeline Gallant

A Dragon's Diary
Dreaming of Dragons

Calling Her Heart
Whisper of the Heart
No Turning Back
Forsake Me Not
Hear My Cry
Calling Her Heart Boxed Set Volumes 1-4

FORGET ME NOT
Victoria, Ontario's Babies 1894 - 1895

Keeper Of Secrets
A Lady's Secret

Midnight's Awakening

Heart of the Storm
Walking Through The Storm
Walking Through The Storm
Heart of the Storm

Secrets of the Underworld
Deklan's Dragons

Tell My Story Collection
Tell My Story: England 1852

The Grave Whisperer
Cataraqui United Church Cemetery
Wedding Bells in Kingston, Ontario, Canada 1923
St. Paul's Anglican Churchyard Kingston, Ontario, Canada A-B
St. Paul's Anglican Churchyard, Kingston, Ontario, Canada C - D
St. Paul's Anglican Churchyard, Kingston, Ontario, Canada G - H
St. Paul's Anglican Churchyard, Kingston, Ontario, Canada J - N
St. Paul's Anglican Churchyard, Kingston, Ontario, Canada O - R
St. Paul's Anglican Churchyard, Kingston, Ontario, Canada S - T
St. Paul's Anglican Churchyard, Kingston, Ontario T - Z
Small Graveyards & Burial Grounds: Kingston, Ontario, Canada
Cataraqui United Church Cemetery 1
Cataraqui United Church Cemetery 2
Cataraqui United Church Cemetary 3
Cataraqui United Church Cemetery 4
Cataraqui United Church Cemetery 5
Beth Israel Cemetery

The Wolf Whisperer Series
The Cry of the Wolf
Captured Heart
Journey of the Heart
Wolf Whisperer volumes 1 & 2
Endless White
The Wolf Whisperer Volumes 1-4
The Wolf Whisperer volumes 1 & 2

Standalone
Winds of Change vol 1-3

Watch for more at https://www.goodreads.com/author/show/
19703964.Angeline_Gallant.